Autism & Girls

Introduction to a Neurodiverse World

Gareth Croot

Contents

Chapter 1: Introduction to Autism in Females

Autism spectrum disorder (ASD) is a neurodevelopmental disorder that affects social communication and interaction, as well as repetitive behaviors and interests. Historically, autism has been characterized as a male-dominated condition, with males being diagnosed at a significantly higher rate than females. However, recent research has suggested that the gender gap in autism may be smaller than previously thought, and that autism may be underdiagnosed in females due to a variety of factors.

In this chapter, we will provide an overview of autism in females, including prevalence rates, symptoms, and challenges faced by females with autism. We will also explore some of the misconceptions and stereotypes surrounding autism in females, and discuss the importance of studying autism from a gender-specific perspective.

Prevalence of Autism in Females

Autism has traditionally been thought of as a male-dominated condition, with estimates of the male-to-female ratio ranging from 2:1 to 5:1. However, recent research has suggested that the true prevalence of autism in females may be higher than previously thought, and that the gender gap may be smaller than initially believed.

One study conducted by the Centers for Disease Control and Prevention (CDC) found that the prevalence of autism in females was approximately 1 in 144, compared to 1 in 54 in males. While this still represents a significant disparity, it suggests that the gap between males and females with autism may not be as wide as previously thought.

Symptoms of Autism in Females

While the core symptoms of autism are the same for both males and females, there are some differences in the way that autism manifests in females. Research has suggested that females with autism may be better able to mask their symptoms in social situations, leading to underdiagnosis and misdiagnosis.

One of the key challenges in diagnosing autism in females is that many of the diagnostic tools and criteria were developed based on male samples. As a result, some of the symptoms that are more common in females with autism may not be included in the diagnostic criteria. For example, females with autism may be more likely to have difficulty with social communication and interaction, but less likely to engage in repetitive behaviors or have restricted interests.

Challenges Faced by Females with Autism

Females with autism face a unique set of challenges that are often overlooked or misunderstood. One of the biggest challenges is social isolation and loneliness, which can be exacerbated by difficulties with social communication and interaction. Females with autism may struggle to form and maintain friendships, which can lead to feelings of loneliness and depression.

Another challenge is the stigma and misconceptions surrounding autism in females. Many people still associate autism primarily with males, and may not recognize the symptoms of autism in females. As a result, females with autism may be misdiagnosed with other conditions, or may not receive a diagnosis at all.

Additionally, females with autism may face discrimination and barriers in education and employment. They may struggle to access the same opportunities and accommodations as their male peers, and may be overlooked for promotions or job opportunities due to their social communication difficulties.

Misconceptions and Stereotypes about Autism in Females

One of the biggest misconceptions about autism in females is that it is a rare condition that primarily affects males. As we have seen, recent research suggests that the prevalence of autism in females may be higher than previously thought, and that many females with autism are underdiagnosed or misdiagnosed.

Another stereotype about autism in females is that it presents in the same way as it does in males. In fact, research has shown that females with autism may be better able to mask their symptoms in social situations, and may have different symptom profiles than males with autism.

Finally, there is a stereotype that autism is a childhood condition that is outgrown in adulthood. While some individuals with autism may experience improvements in symptoms over time, autism is a lifelong condition that affects individuals throughout their lives.

The Importance of Studying Autism from a Gender-Specific Perspective

Given the unique challenges and experiences of females with autism, it is essential that we study autism from a gender-specific perspective. This means not only examining the prevalence and symptoms of autism in females, but also considering the social and cultural factors that may influence diagnosis and treatment.

For example, research has shown that females with autism are more likely to be diagnosed later in life than males, which can delay access to appropriate treatment and support. Understanding the factors that contribute to this delay can help to improve diagnosis and treatment for females with autism.

Similarly, studying autism from a gender-specific perspective can help to identify the unique needs and challenges faced by females with autism. This can inform the development of interventions and support programs that are tailored to the specific needs of this population.

Chapter 2: Gender Differences in Autism

Autism is a neurodevelopmental disorder that affects individuals across the gender spectrum. However, research has shown that there are significant differences in the prevalence, diagnosis, and symptom presentation of autism in males and females. In this chapter, we will explore these gender differences and their implications for diagnosis and treatment.

Prevalence of Autism in Females

Historically, autism has been thought of as a predominantly male disorder, with estimates suggesting that the male-to-female ratio of autism is around 4:1 (Fombonne, 2009). However, recent research has challenged this notion, with studies suggesting that the actual ratio may be closer to 3:1 or even 2:1 (Loomes et al., 2017). Additionally, it has been suggested that autism may be underdiagnosed in females due to the way in which the disorder manifests in females (Lai et al., 2015).

Misconceptions about Autism in Females

One of the biggest misconceptions about autism in females is that it is a rare disorder that primarily affects males. As we have seen, this is not the case, and in fact, there may be a significant number of females with undiagnosed autism. This misconception has led to a lack of research on autism in females and a lack of understanding of the unique challenges faced by females with autism.

Another misconception about autism in females is that it presents in the same way as it does in males. However, research has shown that this is not the case. Females with autism often exhibit different symptoms and behaviors than males with autism, which can lead to misdiagnosis or a delay in diagnosis.

Differences in Diagnosis and Assessment

One of the primary reasons for the underdiagnosis of autism in females is the way in which the disorder is diagnosed and assessed. The diagnostic criteria for autism were developed based on research with male participants, which means that they may not accurately reflect the way in which autism presents in females (Lai et al., 2015).

For example, one of the core diagnostic criteria for autism is a deficit in social communication and interaction. However, research has shown that females with autism may be better at masking their social difficulties than males with autism, which can make it more difficult to diagnose (Lai et al., 2015).

Differences in Symptom Presentation

Research has shown that there are significant differences in the symptom presentation of autism in males and females. While males with autism tend to exhibit more stereotypical behaviors, such as repetitive movements and fixations on specific objects, females with autism often exhibit more subtle and social symptoms (Lai et al., 2015).

For example, females with autism may struggle with social communication and interaction but may be able to mask their difficulties by imitating the behavior of others. This can make it more difficult to diagnose autism in females and can lead to misdiagnosis or a delay in diagnosis.

Gender Bias in Autism Research

The underdiagnosis and misdiagnosis of autism in females can be attributed in part to a gender bias in autism research. Historically, the majority of research on autism has focused on males, which means that our understanding of the disorder is based on a male-centric model.

This bias has led to a lack of research on the unique challenges faced by females with autism and a lack of understanding of the gender-specific symptoms of autism. It is important that we address this bias and begin to conduct research that includes females in order to develop a more accurate understanding of the disorder.

Implications for Diagnosis and Treatment

The gender differences in autism have significant implications for diagnosis and treatment. It is important that healthcare professionals are aware of these differences and are able to identify the unique symptoms of autism in females. This may require a shift in the way that autism is diagnosed and assessed, with a focus on developing more gender-sensitive diagnostic criteria.

Additionally, the gender differences in autism may require different approaches to treatment. For example, females with autism may benefit from social skills training and interventions that focus on communication and interaction. Healthcare professionals should also be aware of the potential for misdiagnosis and should consider the possibility of autism in females who present with symptoms that may not be stereotypically associated with the disorder.

It is also important to address the social and emotional challenges faced by females with autism. Research has shown that females with autism are more likely to experience anxiety and depression than males with autism (Lai et al., 2015). It is important that healthcare professionals provide support for these individuals and help them to develop coping strategies to manage their emotions.

<u>**Chapter 3: Identifying Autism in Females**</u>

Autism spectrum disorder (ASD) is a neurodevelopmental condition characterized by deficits in social communication and interaction, as well as restricted and repetitive patterns of behavior or interests. Historically, autism has been thought of as a predominantly male condition, with the male-to-female ratio estimated to be around 4:1. However, recent research suggests that this ratio may not accurately reflect the true prevalence of autism in females, with many girls and women with autism being undiagnosed or misdiagnosed.

Challenges in identifying autism in females

Identifying autism in females can be challenging for several reasons. One reason is that the diagnostic criteria for autism were originally based on observations of males with the condition, leading to a bias towards identifying autism in males. The symptoms of autism may also present differently in females, with girls and women more likely to exhibit social camouflaging or masking behaviors. Social camouflaging refers to the ability of individuals with autism to imitate social behaviors that may not come naturally to them, making it difficult for others to detect their social deficits. This can result in girls and women with autism being able to "blend in" with their neurotypical peers, and therefore not receiving a diagnosis until later in life, if at all.

Another challenge is the lack of awareness and understanding of autism in females among healthcare professionals, educators, and the general public. This can lead to under-recognition of autism symptoms in females and delays in diagnosis. Additionally, girls and women with autism may present with co-occurring mental health conditions, such as anxiety or depression, which can complicate the diagnostic process and lead to a focus on treating these comorbid conditions rather than addressing the underlying autism.

Commonly missed symptoms in females

There are several symptoms of autism that may be missed in females due to social camouflaging or lack of awareness of the presentation of autism in females. Some commonly missed symptoms include:

1. Social difficulties: Females with autism may struggle with social interactions, but may be able to camouflage their social deficits by imitating social behaviors or adapting to social situations. However, they may still experience social anxiety, feel left out or excluded from social groups, or have difficulty forming and maintaining friendships.

2. Sensory sensitivities: Individuals with autism may have sensory sensitivities, such as being hypersensitive to certain sounds, smells, or textures. In females, these sensitivities may present as discomfort or aversion to certain clothing materials, strong perfumes or scents, or certain types of lighting.

3. Restricted interests: Females with autism may have restricted interests that are different from those typically seen in males with the condition. For example, they may be more interested in animals, art, or literature, rather than the stereotypical interests of males with autism, such as trains or computers.

4. Repetitive behaviors: Individuals with autism may engage in repetitive behaviors or routines, such as lining up objects, repeating words or phrases, or engaging in stereotypic movements. In females, these behaviors may present as an adherence to rigid routines or a need for symmetry or order.

Diagnostic tools for autism in females

There are several diagnostic tools that can be used to identify autism in females, including standardized diagnostic assessments, developmental screenings, and observational assessments.

The gold standard for diagnosing autism is the Diagnostic and Statistical Manual of Mental Disorders (DSM), currently in its fifth edition (DSM-5). The DSM-5 includes specific criteria for diagnosing autism, including deficits in social communication and interaction, restricted and repetitive behaviors or interests, and symptom onset in early childhood. However, as mentioned previously, these criteria were developed based on observations of males with autism and may not accurately reflect the presentation of autism in females.

Another tool that may be useful in identifying autism in females is developmental screenings. Developmental screenings are brief assessments that can be completed by healthcare providers or educators to identify children who may be at risk for developmental delays or disorders, including autism. These screenings typically include questions about the child's communication, social skills, and behavior. While developmental screenings are not diagnostic, they can help identify children who may need further evaluation for autism.

Observational assessments are also an important tool in identifying autism in females. Observational assessments involve observing the child's behavior and interactions in various settings, such as at home, school, or during playtime. These assessments can provide valuable information about the child's social communication, play skills, and repetitive behaviors, which can help inform a diagnosis of autism.

In addition to these diagnostic tools, it is important for healthcare providers and educators to be aware of the presentation of autism in females and to consider the possibility of autism when girls or women present with symptoms that may not fit the traditional male presentation of the condition.

The importance of early diagnosis and intervention
Early diagnosis and intervention are crucial for individuals with autism, regardless of gender. Early intervention can help improve outcomes and increase the likelihood of positive long-term outcomes, such as improved social communication, academic achievement, and quality of life. However, because autism in females may be under-recognized or misdiagnosed, many girls and women with autism may not receive a diagnosis until later in life, if at all.

Late diagnosis can result in missed opportunities for early intervention and support, leading to greater challenges in social communication, academic achievement, and mental health. Therefore, it is important for healthcare providers, educators, and the general public to be aware of the presentation of autism in females and to consider the possibility of autism in girls and women who may be exhibiting symptoms.

Chapter 4: Co-occurring Conditions in Autism

Autism is often accompanied by other medical and mental health conditions, known as co-occurring conditions or comorbidities. These conditions can vary widely in their severity and impact on an individual with autism, but they can significantly affect quality of life and daily functioning. In this chapter, we will explore the prevalence of co-occurring conditions in individuals with autism, with a focus on how these conditions may differ in females compared to males.

Prevalence of Co-occurring Conditions

Research has shown that individuals with autism are more likely to have one or more co-occurring conditions than individuals without autism. A study conducted by the Centers for Disease Control and Prevention (CDC) found that 39% of children with autism had at least one co-occurring condition, while 14% had two or more. Common co-occurring conditions in autism include:

Intellectual disability: This is the most common co-occurring condition in autism, affecting 31% of individuals with autism according to the CDC study. Intellectual disability is characterized by significant limitations in intellectual functioning and adaptive behaviors, such as communication and daily living skills.

Attention deficit hyperactivity disorder (ADHD): ADHD is a common condition that affects an individual's ability to focus, control impulsive behaviors, and sit still. According to the CDC study, 29% of children with autism also had ADHD.

Anxiety: Anxiety disorders are characterized by excessive and persistent worry or fear, often leading to avoidance behaviors. Anxiety is common in individuals with autism, with studies estimating that up to 40% of individuals with autism also have an anxiety disorder.

Depression: Depression is a mood disorder characterized by feelings of sadness, hopelessness, and loss of interest in activities. Research has found that individuals with autism have higher rates of depression than the general population.

Gastrointestinal (GI) disorders: GI disorders such as constipation, diarrhea, and gastroesophageal reflux disease (GERD) are common in individuals with autism, with studies estimating that up to 70% of individuals with autism experience GI symptoms.

Co-occurring Conditions in Females with Autism

While research on co-occurring conditions in autism has primarily focused on males, recent studies have begun to investigate how these conditions may differ in females. One study found that females with autism are more likely to have anxiety, depression, and sleep disorders than males with autism. Another study found that females with autism are more likely to have eating disorders and self-injurious behaviors than males with autism.

One potential reason for these gender differences is that females with autism may be more skilled at masking their symptoms and appearing socially "normal," leading to delayed diagnosis and a greater risk for developing co-occurring conditions. In addition, females may be subjected to greater societal pressure to conform to gender expectations, leading to increased stress and anxiety.

Addressing Co-occurring Conditions

Addressing co-occurring conditions is an important aspect of treating individuals with autism. While there is no one-size-fits-all approach to treating co-occurring conditions, there are several evidence-based treatments and interventions that can be effective for individuals with autism:

Behavioral interventions: Behavioral interventions such as applied behavior analysis (ABA) and cognitive-behavioral therapy (CBT) have been shown to be effective for treating anxiety, depression, and other co-occurring conditions in individuals with autism.

Medications: Medications such as antidepressants and antipsychotics can be effective for treating anxiety, depression, and other co-occurring conditions in individuals with autism. However, medication should be used cautiously and under the supervision of a healthcare provider, as individuals with autism may be more sensitive to the side effects of medication.

Dietary interventions: Some individuals with autism may benefit from dietary interventions, such as a gluten-free or casein-free diet, to address gastrointestinal symptoms or improve behavior.

Occupational therapy: Occupational therapy can be helpful for addressing sensory processing difficulties and improving daily living skills in individuals with autism.

Speech therapy: Speech therapy can be helpful for addressing communication difficulties in individuals with autism, which can in turn improve social skills and reduce anxiety.

It is important to note that co-occurring conditions can often be overlooked or misdiagnosed in individuals with autism, particularly in females who may be better at masking their symptoms. Therefore, it is essential for healthcare providers to screen for and address co-occurring conditions in individuals with autism.

Chapter 5: Psychological and Emotional Effects of Autism in Females

Autism is often thought of as a purely neurological disorder, but it can also have significant psychological and emotional effects. These effects can be especially pronounced in females, who often face unique challenges due to gender expectations and societal norms. In this chapter, we will explore some of the most common psychological and emotional effects of autism in females and discuss strategies for addressing these challenges.

Common Emotional Challenges Faced by Females with Autism:

One of the most common emotional challenges faced by females with autism is social isolation and loneliness. Social communication difficulties, a hallmark symptom of autism, can make it difficult for females to form and maintain meaningful friendships and relationships. This can lead to feelings of loneliness, depression, and anxiety. In addition, females with autism may feel misunderstood or rejected by their peers, which can further exacerbate these feelings.

Another emotional challenge faced by females with autism is anxiety. Females with autism often experience anxiety in social situations due to their difficulties with social communication and sensory processing. They may also struggle with generalized anxiety related to their worries about the future or their inability to cope with change.

Depression is another common emotional challenge faced by females with autism. This may be due in part to the social isolation and anxiety that often accompany the disorder, but it may also be related to the challenges of navigating a world that is not designed for individuals with autism. The prevalence of depression in females with autism may be higher than in males, but more research is needed to fully understand this relationship.

Social Isolation and Loneliness:

Social isolation and loneliness are significant issues for many females with autism. These challenges can have a significant impact on mental health and well-being. Therefore, it is important to address these challenges through the development of social skills and strategies for building and maintaining relationships.

One approach to addressing social isolation and loneliness in females with autism is through the development of social skills training programs. These programs focus on teaching individuals with autism how to communicate effectively with others, read social cues, and develop relationships. They may also include strategies for managing anxiety in social situations.

Another approach to addressing social isolation and loneliness is through the creation of inclusive social environments. This may include developing programs and activities that are designed to be accessible to individuals with autism, such as sensory-friendly events or activities that focus on shared interests. It may also involve educating peers and community members about autism and creating a more welcoming and accepting environment for individuals with the disorder.

Anxiety:

Anxiety is another significant emotional challenge faced by many females with autism. Anxiety in social situations is particularly common, but individuals with autism may also experience generalized anxiety related to worries about the future or their ability to cope with change.

One approach to addressing anxiety in females with autism is through the use of cognitive-behavioral therapy (CBT). CBT is a type of therapy that focuses on changing negative thought patterns and developing coping strategies for managing anxiety. This type of therapy can be particularly effective for individuals with autism, as it provides concrete strategies for managing anxiety in social situations and can help to build confidence and self-esteem.

Another approach to addressing anxiety in females with autism is through the use of medication. Selective serotonin reuptake inhibitors (SSRIs) and other medications may be effective in managing anxiety in individuals with autism, but it is important to work closely with a healthcare provider to ensure that the medication is safe and effective.

Depression:

Depression is another significant emotional challenge faced by many females with autism. This may be due in part to the social isolation and anxiety that often accompany the disorder, but it may also be related to the challenges of navigating a world that is not designed for individuals with autism.

One approach to addressing depression in females with autism is through the use of therapy. Cognitive-behavior al therapy (CBT) and other forms of talk therapy can be effective in treating depression in individuals with autism. These therapies can help individuals to identify and challenge negative thought patterns and develop strategies for coping with the challenges of the disorder.

Another approach to addressing depression in females with autism is through the use of medication. Antidepressants may be effective in treating depression in individuals with autism, but it is important to work closely with a healthcare provider to ensure that the medication is safe and effective.

Self-Esteem and Identity:

Self-esteem and identity can also be significant challenges for females with autism. The unique challenges of the disorder, as well as the societal expectations placed on women and girls, can make it difficult for individuals with autism to develop a strong sense of self and feel confident in their abilities.

One approach to addressing self-esteem and identity in females with autism is through the use of therapy. CBT and other forms of talk therapy can be effective in helping individuals to develop a more positive self-image and build confidence in their abilities. Therapists can also help individuals to identify their strengths and develop strategies for leveraging these strengths in their daily lives.

Another approach to addressing self-esteem and identity in females with autism is through the development of supportive social networks. This may include finding and connecting with other individuals with autism, as well as developing relationships with supportive family members, friends, and community members.

Chapter 6: Neurodevelopmental Differences in Autism in Females

Autism is a neurodevelopmental disorder that affects individuals in a variety of ways, including social communication, behavior, and sensory processing. However, the way that autism presents in females can be different than in males. In this chapter, we will explore the neurodevelopmental differences in autism in females and how they can impact the way that autism is diagnosed and treated.

Differences in Brain Development

Research has shown that females with autism have differences in brain development compared to males with autism and neurotypical females. For example, studies have found that the amygdala, which is responsible for processing emotions, is larger in females with autism than in males with autism or neurotypical females. Additionally, there may be differences in the connectivity between different regions of the brain in females with autism.

These differences in brain development may contribute to the way that autism presents in females. For example, females with autism may have better language abilities than males with autism, which could be related to differences in the development of certain brain regions. However, it is important to note that these differences in brain development are not universal and can vary widely among individuals with autism.

Differences in Sensory Processing

Sensory processing is another area in which females with autism may differ from males with autism. Research has found that females with autism are more likely to have sensory processing difficulties, such as being hypersensitive to sounds or textures. These sensory processing difficulties can be very challenging for females with autism and can impact their ability to participate in daily activities.

One possible explanation for these differences in sensory processing is that females may be more likely to mask their sensory difficulties. In other words, females may learn to hide their sensory processing difficulties in order to fit in with their peers. This can make it more difficult for females with autism to receive the support and accommodations that they need.

Implications for Intervention and Treatment

Understanding the neurodevelopmental differences in autism in females can have important implications for intervention and treatment. For example, research has suggested that females with autism may be more responsive to social interventions than males with autism. This may be related to the fact that females with autism may have better language abilities and be more motivated to socialize.

Additionally, understanding the differences in sensory processing can help clinicians and therapists to tailor interventions to meet the unique needs of females with autism. For example, providing sensory accommodations, such as noise-cancelling headphones or weighted blankets, can help females with autism to better cope with sensory stimuli.

It is also important to note that the traditional diagnostic criteria for autism may not accurately capture the way that autism presents in females. The diagnostic criteria were developed based on research with males with autism, and may not fully capture the way that autism presents in females. For example, females with autism may be better able to mask their difficulties with social communication, which could result in a missed diagnosis or a misdiagnosis of another condition.

Therefore, it is important for clinicians to be aware of the potential differences in the way that autism presents in females and to take a comprehensive and individualized approach to diagnosis and treatment.

Chapter 7: Educational Needs of Females with Autism

Education plays a crucial role in the development of individuals with autism. It is particularly important for females with autism, who may face unique challenges in the educational system. In this chapter, we will explore the educational needs of females with autism and strategies to support their academic success.

Challenges in Educational Settings:

Females with autism may face numerous challenges in educational settings. These challenges can include difficulty with social interaction, communication, and sensory processing. Females with autism may also have a narrow range of interests, which can make it challenging to engage them in traditional academic subjects. They may also struggle with executive functioning skills, such as time management and organization.

In addition to these challenges, females with autism may also experience gender bias in the educational system. Research has shown that girls with autism are often misdiagnosed or diagnosed later than boys with autism, which can delay their access to appropriate support and accommodations. They may also face stereotyping and discrimination from teachers and peers who have a limited understanding of autism in females.

Strategies to Support Learning and Academic Success:

Despite these challenges, there are strategies that can be implemented to support the learning and academic success of females with autism.

Individualized Education Plans (IEPs):

Individualized Education Plans (IEPs) are a legal requirement for students with disabilities, including autism. An IEP is a written plan that outlines the student's strengths, needs, and goals, as well as the supports and accommodations that will be provided to help them achieve those goals. An IEP is developed by a team that includes the student's parents, teachers, and other educational professionals. The plan is reviewed and updated annually to ensure that it is meeting the student's changing needs.

IEPs are particularly important for females with autism because they can help to ensure that their unique needs and strengths are taken into account in the educational setting. For example, an IEP may include accommodations such as sensory breaks, extended time on assignments, and visual aids to support learning.

Inclusive Classrooms:

Inclusive classrooms are another strategy that can benefit females with autism. An inclusive classroom is one in which students with disabilities learn alongside their non-disabled peers. This can provide opportunities for social interaction and inclusion, which can be particularly beneficial for females with autism who may struggle with social skills.

Inclusive classrooms can also provide opportunities for differentiation, which is the practice of tailoring instruction to meet the individual needs of each student. For example, a teacher may provide different types of assignments or activities to engage students with a range of interests and abilities.

Visual Aids and Assistive Technology:

Visual aids and assistive technology can be powerful tools for supporting the learning and academic success of females with autism. Visual aids, such as pictures, diagrams, and charts, can help to make abstract concepts more concrete and understandable. Assistive technology, such as text-to-speech software and speech-to-text software, can help to support communication and written expression.

These tools can be particularly beneficial for females with autism who may struggle with language and communication skills. They can help to reduce frustration and improve engagement in academic subjects.

Social Skills Training:

Social skills training is another strategy that can support the academic success of females with autism. Social skills training can include instruction on topics such as communication, social interaction, and emotional regulation. It can also provide opportunities for social practice and feedback.

Social skills training can be particularly beneficial for females with autism who may struggle with social interaction and making friends. It can also help to reduce anxiety and improve self-confidence.

Advocacy and Support:

Advocacy and support are critical for ensuring that females with autism receive the educational support and accommodations that they need to succeed. Parents, caregivers, and educators can play an important role in advocating for the needs of females with autism and ensuring that they receive appropriate support and accommodations.

Advocacy can include requesting an IEP or other accommodations, working with teachers and school administrators to ensure that the educational environment is supportive and inclusive, and seeking out resources and support from community organizations and advocacy groups.

In addition to advocacy, support from caregivers and educators is also critical for the academic success of females with autism. This can include providing emotional support and encouragement, helping with homework and organization, and providing opportunities for socialization and community involvement.

Chapter 8: Transition to Adulthood

Transitioning from adolescence to adulthood can be a challenging time for anyone, but for individuals with autism, this period can be especially difficult. As individuals with autism reach adulthood, they are faced with a new set of challenges, such as finding employment, living independently, and building social connections. Females with autism may face additional barriers due to gender-based expectations and societal stereotypes. In this chapter, we will explore the unique challenges that females with autism face during the transition to adulthood and the support and resources available to help them succeed.

Challenges Faced by Females with Autism

As females with autism move into adulthood, they may experience a variety of challenges that can make the transition more difficult. For example, they may struggle with building social connections and maintaining friendships, finding employment, and living independently. Females with autism may also face additional barriers related to gender, such as societal expectations around femininity and the perception that autism primarily affects males.

Social Challenges

Building and maintaining social connections can be especially challenging for females with autism. This is due in part to the fact that females with autism may have different social needs and interests than their male counterparts. For example, they may be more interested in forming close, intimate relationships with a smaller group of friends rather than participating in large group activities. Females with autism may also have difficulty understanding social cues, interpreting nonverbal communication, and expressing their own emotions.

Employment Challenges

Finding and maintaining employment can be a major challenge for individuals with autism, and this is especially true for females. Females with autism may struggle to find jobs that match their skills and interests, and they may face discrimination in the workplace based on both their gender and their autism. In addition, females with autism may have difficulty navigating the complex social dynamics of the workplace and may need additional support and accommodations to succeed.

Independent Living Challenges

Living independently can be a daunting prospect for anyone, but it can be especially challenging for individuals with autism. Females with autism may face additional barriers related to societal expectations around femininity, such as the assumption that they will have a caregiver or spouse to help them with daily tasks. In addition, females with autism may have difficulty with practical skills such as managing money, cooking, and cleaning.

Support and Resources

Despite the challenges that females with autism may face during the transition to adulthood, there are many support and resources available to help them succeed. In this section, we will explore some of the key resources that can help females with autism during the transition to adulthood.

Education and Training

Education and training can be an important tool for helping females with autism prepare for the transition to adulthood. For example, vocational training programs can provide individuals with autism with the skills they need to find and maintain employment. Social skills training programs can also help individuals with autism build the social connections they need to succeed in the workplace and in other areas of life.

Mentorship and Role Models

Having a mentor or role model can be an important source of support for females with autism during the transition to adulthood. A mentor or role model can provide guidance, support, and encouragement, and can help individuals with autism build the skills and confidence they need to succeed. Mentors and role models can come from a variety of sources, including family members, teachers, and community organizations.

Advocacy and Support Groups

Advocacy and support groups can provide individuals with autism and their families with a range of resources and support during the transition to adulthood. These groups can help individuals with autism access services and supports, navigate the challenges of the transition to adulthood, and connect with others who share their experiences. Support groups can also provide a safe and welcoming space for individuals with autism to share their thoughts and feelings, and to receive support and encouragement from others who understand their struggles.

Accommodations and Services

There are a variety of accommodations and services available to individuals with autism that can help them succeed during the transition to adulthood. For example, individuals with autism may be eligible for accommodations in the workplace, such as a quiet workspace or flexible scheduling. They may also be eligible for services such as occupational therapy, speech therapy, or counseling, which can help them develop the skills they need to succeed in different areas of life.

Chapter 9: Employment and Career Development

Females with autism face unique challenges in employment and career development due to their neurodivergent traits and gender biases in the workplace. Employment can be an essential component of independence, financial stability, and self-esteem, and individuals with autism should have equal opportunities to pursue their career aspirations. In this chapter, we will explore the challenges faced by females with autism in the workplace and discuss strategies for success and the importance of inclusive hiring practices.

Challenges faced by Females with Autism in the Workplace:

Females with autism face several barriers in the workplace, such as difficulties with social communication, sensory sensitivities, and executive function skills. These challenges can affect their ability to perform specific job duties and interact effectively with co-workers and supervisors. Moreover, gender biases can negatively affect how females with autism are perceived and evaluated in the workplace, leading to discrimination and exclusion.

One significant challenge for females with autism is the lack of understanding and accommodations for their neurodivergent traits. Many employers may not be aware of the unique needs of individuals with autism or may not know how to provide appropriate support. Additionally, females with autism may struggle with job interviews, which can be particularly challenging for individuals with social communication difficulties. These individuals may not be able to effectively convey their skills and experiences, leading to missed opportunities.

Another significant challenge is the lack of representation and role models for females with autism in the workplace. Female representation in executive positions is low, making it difficult for females with autism to find role models who can provide guidance and mentorship. Additionally, the underrepresentation of females with autism in the workplace can lead to a lack of awareness and understanding of their unique strengths and abilities.

Strategies for Success:

Despite the challenges faced by females with autism in the workplace, several strategies can promote success and help individuals with autism thrive in their careers. One essential strategy is self-advocacy, where individuals with autism communicate their needs and strengths to their employers and colleagues. Self-advocacy can help individuals with autism receive accommodations and support that will allow them to perform their job duties effectively.

Another strategy is to find a mentor or role model who can provide guidance and support. A mentor can help individuals with autism navigate the workplace and provide advice on career development and advancement. Additionally, finding a community of peers with autism can provide a sense of belonging and support.

Employers can also play a vital role in promoting success for employees with autism. Inclusive hiring practices, such as providing job descriptions that are clear and easy to understand, can help individuals with autism apply for jobs that align with their strengths and skills. Additionally, employers can provide accommodations, such as flexible work schedules or sensory-friendly workspaces, to help individuals with autism work more comfortably and productively.

Importance of Inclusive Hiring Practices:

Inclusive hiring practices are crucial for promoting diversity and providing equal opportunities for individuals with autism. Employers who value inclusivity and diversity are more likely to attract and retain employees with autism, who may bring unique perspectives and talents to the workplace. Additionally, inclusive hiring practices can help break down stereotypes and stigmas surrounding individuals with autism and promote a more inclusive and accepting workplace culture.

One example of inclusive hiring practices is the "Autism at Work" program, launched by several companies such as Microsoft and SAP. This program provides training and support for employees with autism and promotes inclusive hiring practices, such as alternative interview formats and accommodations in the workplace. Through these initiatives, these companies have shown that individuals with autism can thrive in the workplace with the right support and accommodations.

Chapter 10: Relationships and Social Skills

Building and maintaining relationships is a key aspect of human life, but it can be challenging for individuals with autism, particularly females. Autism is often characterized by social communication deficits and difficulty with social interactions, which can make it difficult for individuals with autism to form and maintain relationships. However, with the right support and strategies, individuals with autism can develop social skills and build meaningful relationships.

Challenges Faced by Females with Autism in Social Situations

Females with autism face unique challenges in social situations, which can make it difficult to form and maintain relationships. For example, females with autism may struggle with understanding social cues and social norms, which can make it difficult to interpret others' intentions and emotions accurately. Additionally, females with autism may have difficulty with initiating and maintaining conversations, which can lead to social isolation and difficulty forming friendships. This can be especially challenging during adolescence, a time when social interactions become increasingly important.

Inclusive Social Environments

Creating inclusive social environments is an important step in supporting individuals with autism in building relationships. Inclusive social environments are those that promote understanding, acceptance, and inclusivity of individuals with disabilities, including autism. These environments can be created in a variety of settings, such as schools, community centers, and social clubs.

One strategy for creating inclusive social environments is to provide opportunities for individuals with autism to engage in social activities with their peers. For example, social clubs or groups that focus on shared interests or hobbies can provide a safe and supportive environment for individuals with autism to meet and interact with others who share their interests. Inclusive social activities can also be integrated into school or work settings, such as group projects or team-building activities.

Improving Social Skills

Social skills training is a common intervention used to help individuals with autism develop social skills and build relationships. Social skills training can be delivered in a variety of settings, such as school, therapy, or community-based programs. The goal of social skills training is to teach individuals with autism the skills they need to engage in social interactions successfully.

One common approach to social skills training is role-playing. Role-playing involves simulating social situations and practicing appropriate social behaviors, such as initiating and maintaining conversations, making eye contact, and interpreting social cues. Role-playing can be done individually or in a group setting, and it can be tailored to the individual's specific needs.

Another strategy for improving social skills is peer-mediated interventions. Peer-mediated interventions involve pairing individuals with autism with typically developing peers who serve as social partners and role models. The typically developing peers can model appropriate social behaviors, provide feedback and reinforcement, and help individuals with autism practice social skills in a naturalistic setting.

Social Stories

Social stories are a visual intervention that can be used to help individuals with autism understand social situations and develop appropriate social behaviors. Social stories are brief, illustrated stories that describe social situations and the expected social behaviors. They can be used to teach individuals with autism about social norms and help them understand social cues and expectations.

Social stories can be tailored to the individual's specific needs and can be used in a variety of settings, such as school, therapy, or home. For example, a social story might be created to help an individual with autism understand how to initiate a conversation with a peer. The story might include illustrations of appropriate social behaviors, such as making eye contact, smiling, and asking questions.

Relationship Building

Building and maintaining relationships requires effort and practice, and individuals with autism may need additional support to develop these skills successfully. One strategy for building relationships is to focus on shared interests or hobbies. Shared interests can provide a foundation for social interactions and can help individuals with autism feel more comfortable in social situations.

Another strategy is to focus on building social skills gradually, starting with simple social interactions and gradually building up to more complex interactions. For example, an individual with autism might start by practicing greeting others or asking simple questions, and then gradually move on to more complex social behaviors, such as initiating a conversation or participating in group activities.

It's also important to recognize that building relationships takes time and effort. Individuals with autism may need additional support and patience from family members, friends, and social partners as they work to develop their social skills and build relationships.

Supporting Individuals with Autism in Romantic Relationships

Individuals with autism may also face unique challenges in romantic relationships. For example, they may struggle with understanding social cues and reading their partner's emotions, which can make it difficult to navigate romantic situations successfully. Additionally, individuals with autism may have difficulty with intimacy and expressing their emotions, which can make it challenging to build and maintain romantic relationships.

However, with the right support and strategies, individuals with autism can develop the skills they need to engage in romantic relationships successfully. Some strategies for supporting individuals with autism in romantic relationships include:

Providing education about social norms and expectations in romantic relationships.
Encouraging open communication and providing support for individuals with autism to express their emotions and needs.
Focusing on shared interests and activities as a way to build a foundation for the relationship.

Providing support and guidance for navigating difficult social situations, such as conflicts or misunderstandings.

Having a child with autism can have a profound impact on the family unit. Parents and caregivers face unique challenges in raising a daughter with autism, and the entire family may need additional support to navigate the many complexities of this condition.

In this chapter, we will explore the challenges faced by families with a daughter with autism, strategies for supporting the family unit, and the importance of self-care for parents and caregivers.

Challenges Faced by Families

Parents of children with autism often experience significant stress, anxiety, and depression. The additional demands of raising a child with autism can be overwhelming, and the lack of understanding and support from others can exacerbate these challenges.

For families with a daughter with autism, there may be additional challenges related to gender. Autism is often perceived as a condition that affects males more than females, and as a result, girls with autism may be overlooked or misdiagnosed. This can lead to delayed diagnosis and treatment, which can have a negative impact on the entire family.

Families may also face challenges related to communication and social skills. Children with autism may struggle to communicate their needs and feelings, which can be frustrating for both the child and the parent. They may also have difficulty making and maintaining friendships, which can lead to social isolation and loneliness.

Strategies for Supporting the Family Unit

Despite these challenges, there are many strategies that parents and caregivers can use to support the family unit. Some of these strategies include:

1. Education and Advocacy: Parents and caregivers can educate themselves about autism and advocate for their child's needs. By understanding the condition and the available resources, they can make informed decisions about treatment and support.

2. Communication: Communication is key in any relationship, and it is especially important in families with a child with autism. Parents and caregivers can work with their child's therapist to develop communication strategies that work for the whole family. This may include using visual aids, such as pictures or symbols, to help the child communicate their needs and feelings.

3. Self-Care: Taking care of oneself is crucial when caring for a child with autism. Parents and caregivers can benefit from support groups, therapy, and respite care to help manage stress and prevent burnout.

4. Family Therapy: Family therapy can be beneficial for families with a child with autism. This type of therapy focuses on improving communication, reducing stress, and strengthening family relationships.

5. Specialized Services: There are many specialized services available for families with a child with autism, including respite care, in-home therapy, and support groups. These services can provide much-needed support and respite for parents and caregivers.

Importance of Self-Care for Parents and Caregivers
Self-care is critical for parents and caregivers of children with autism. The demands of caring for a child with autism can be overwhelming, and it is easy to neglect one's own needs in the process. However, neglecting one's own needs can lead to burnout and increased stress.

Some self-care strategies that parents and caregivers can use include:

1. Exercise: Exercise is a great way to reduce stress and improve overall health. Parents and caregivers can find ways to incorporate exercise into their daily routine, such as taking a walk during their child's therapy session.

2. Hobbies: Engaging in hobbies and activities that bring joy and fulfillment can be a great way to reduce stress and improve mental health. Parents and caregivers can make time for activities they enjoy, such as reading, gardening, or painting.

3. Respite Care: Respite care is temporary care provided to a child
    with autism so that their parents or caregivers can take a break.
    This can be a great way for parents and caregivers to recharge and
    practice self-care.

4. Therapy: Therapy can be beneficial for parents and caregivers of
    children with autism. It can provide a safe space to process
    emotions and develop coping strategies for managing stress.

5. Support Groups: Support groups can be a great way to connect
    with other parents and caregivers who are going through similar
    experiences. They can provide a sense of community and support,
    as well as opportunities for education and advocacy.

Chapter 12: Cultural and Ethnic Diversity in Autism

Autism is a neurodevelopmental disorder that affects individuals from all walks of life, regardless of culture, ethnicity, or socioeconomic status. However, there are disparities in the diagnosis and treatment of autism across cultures, highlighting the importance of understanding and addressing cultural and ethnic diversity in autism.

Differences in Diagnosis and Treatment Across Cultures

Research has shown that there are differences in the diagnosis and treatment of autism across cultures. For example, studies have found that individuals from certain cultures, such as Asian and Hispanic cultures, are less likely to receive an autism diagnosis compared to individuals from Western cultures (Mandell et al., 2009). This may be due to differences in cultural beliefs and attitudes towards autism, as well as variations in the availability and accessibility of diagnostic services.

Cultural beliefs and attitudes towards disability can also impact the way autism is perceived and treated within a culture. In some cultures, disability is stigmatized and seen as a personal failing or punishment, while in others, disability is viewed as a natural part of life and accepted as such. These cultural beliefs can influence the way autism is perceived and treated within a culture, with some cultures placing a greater emphasis on addressing symptoms and others focusing on acceptance and accommodation.

Additionally, variations in the availability and accessibility of diagnostic services can impact the diagnosis of autism in different cultures. In some cultures, there may be a lack of awareness of autism and its symptoms, which can lead to a delay in diagnosis or misdiagnosis. Access to diagnostic services may also be limited in certain areas, making it difficult for individuals to receive an accurate diagnosis and access appropriate treatment.

Importance of Cultural Sensitivity and Competence

Understanding and addressing cultural and ethnic diversity in autism is essential for ensuring that individuals receive the care and support they need. This includes developing cultural sensitivity and competence among healthcare professionals, educators, and other service providers.

Cultural sensitivity involves being aware of and respectful towards different cultures and their beliefs, values, and practices. It also involves recognizing the impact that culture can have on the way individuals perceive and respond to their symptoms, as well as their attitudes towards seeking treatment.

Cultural competence takes cultural sensitivity a step further, involving the ability to effectively navigate cultural differences and provide appropriate care and support to individuals from diverse backgrounds. This may involve adapting interventions to better align with cultural beliefs and practices, as well as working collaboratively with families and communities to address cultural barriers and promote understanding.

Strategies for Promoting Inclusivity and Diversity

There are several strategies that can be employed to promote inclusivity and diversity in the diagnosis and treatment of autism. These include:

Providing culturally sensitive and competent diagnostic services - This may involve offering diagnostic services in multiple languages, adapting diagnostic tools to better align with cultural beliefs and practices, and training clinicians in cultural sensitivity and competence.

Engaging with families and communities - Engaging with families and communities can help to promote understanding and acceptance of autism, as well as identify and address cultural barriers to diagnosis and treatment.

Adapting interventions to better align with cultural beliefs and practices - This may involve incorporating traditional healing practices and beliefs into treatment, as well as working with families and communities to identify culturally appropriate interventions.

Raising awareness of autism in diverse communities - Raising awareness of autism in diverse communities can help to increase understanding and acceptance of the disorder, as well as promote early identification and intervention.

Addressing disparities in access to diagnostic and treatment services - Addressing disparities in access to diagnostic and treatment services can help to ensure that individuals from all backgrounds have access to the care and support they need.

Chapter 13: Autism and Menstruation

Autism spectrum disorder (ASD) is a neurodevelopmental condition that affects social communication and behavior. Females with ASD face unique challenges related to their gender and diagnosis, including the impact of their condition on menstruation.

The impact of autism on menstruation can vary depending on the individual, but many females with ASD experience difficulties related to hormonal changes and the physical and emotional symptoms of menstruation.

Challenges Faced by Females with Autism during Menstruation

Hormonal changes during menstruation can affect mood, behavior, and sensory processing in females with ASD. This can lead to increased anxiety, irritability, and sensitivity to sensory stimuli. Many females with ASD also struggle with executive functioning and may find it difficult to manage the practical aspects of menstruation, such as tracking their menstrual cycle and using pads or tampons.

In addition, females with ASD may struggle with communication and social interaction related to menstruation. They may find it difficult to express their needs or concerns related to menstruation, or may feel embarrassed or ashamed to discuss it with others. This can lead to feelings of isolation and anxiety.

Finally, females with ASD may experience co-occurring conditions that can exacerbate the challenges of menstruation. For example, individuals with gastrointestinal issues or chronic pain may experience worsening symptoms during menstruation, leading to increased discomfort and distress.

Strategies for Managing Menstrual Symptoms

There are several strategies that can help females with ASD manage the challenges of menstruation:

Education and Awareness: Education and awareness are key to supporting females with ASD during menstruation. Girls and women with ASD should be provided with information about menstrual health, including the physical and emotional changes associated with menstruation and practical tips for managing symptoms.

Visual Supports: Visual supports such as social stories and visual schedules can be helpful in preparing girls and women with ASD for menstruation. These tools can help individuals understand what to expect and how to manage their symptoms.

Sensory Supports: Sensory supports such as weighted blankets, noise-canceling headphones, and fidget toys can help females with ASD manage sensory sensitivities during menstruation.

Executive Functioning Supports: Females with ASD may benefit from supports to help with executive functioning, such as checklists or reminders for tracking their menstrual cycle and managing menstrual products.

Communication Supports: It is important to provide females with ASD with opportunities to communicate their needs and concerns related to menstruation. This may involve using alternative modes of communication such as visual supports or assistive technology.

Medical Supports: Females with ASD should receive appropriate medical supports for managing menstrual symptoms. This may include medication for pain or hormonal imbalances, as well as accommodations such as flexible work or school schedules to manage symptoms.

Importance of Education and Awareness

Education and awareness are critical for supporting females with ASD during menstruation. Many girls and women with ASD may not have access to accurate information about menstrual health, and may struggle to understand and manage their symptoms as a result.

Providing education and awareness about menstruation can help to reduce anxiety and increase confidence in managing symptoms. It can also help to reduce stigma and promote a more inclusive and accepting environment for individuals with ASD.

Education and awareness should be provided in a way that is accessible and tailored to the individual's needs. This may involve using visual supports, simplified language, or assistive technology to convey information.

Importance of Addressing Co-Occurring Conditions

Many females with ASD experience co-occurring conditions that can exacerbate the challenges of menstruation. Addressing these conditions is critical for promoting overall health and well-being.

For example, females with ASD who experience chronic pain or gastrointestinal issues may benefit from medical treatment or dietary changes to manage their symptoms. Similarly, individuals with anxiety or depression may benefit from counseling or medication to manage their emotional symptoms.

It is important for healthcare providers to screen for co-occurring conditions and provide appropriate treatment and support. This may involve working with a multidisciplinary team of healthcare providers, including psychologists, gastroenterologists, and pain specialists.

In addition, addressing co-occurring conditions may require accommodations or modifications to menstrual management strategies. For example, an individual with chronic pain may need to use a different type of menstrual product or adjust their menstrual management schedule to reduce discomfort.

Importance of Support Networks

Support networks are critical for promoting the health and well-being of females with ASD during menstruation. These networks may include family members, friends, teachers, healthcare providers, and support groups.

Support networks can provide emotional support, practical advice, and a sense of community for individuals with ASD. They can also help to reduce stigma and promote acceptance of differences.

It is important for females with ASD to identify and engage with supportive individuals and organizations. This may involve joining a support group for individuals with ASD, talking with a trusted family member or friend, or working with a healthcare provider who is knowledgeable about ASD.

Chapter 14: Healthcare and Medical Needs

Individuals with autism spectrum disorder (ASD) often have a range of healthcare and medical needs that require specialized care. This is especially true for females with ASD, who may face unique challenges in accessing appropriate healthcare services. In this chapter, we will discuss some of the common healthcare and medical needs of females with ASD and the strategies for addressing these needs.

Co-occurring Medical Conditions in Females with Autism

Individuals with ASD are more likely to have co-occurring medical conditions compared to the general population. In females with ASD, some of the common co-occurring medical conditions include gastrointestinal problems, epilepsy, sleep disorders, and allergies. These conditions can significantly impact the quality of life and overall health of individuals with ASD.

Gastrointestinal (GI) problems are one of the most common co-occurring medical conditions in individuals with ASD, and females with ASD are more likely to have GI problems compared to males with ASD. Symptoms of GI problems in females with ASD can include abdominal pain, constipation, diarrhea, and vomiting. It is important to note that GI problems can often be linked to dietary and nutritional factors, as well as sensory processing issues.

Epilepsy is another co-occurring medical condition that is more common in individuals with ASD compared to the general population. Females with ASD are more likely to have epilepsy compared to males with ASD. Epilepsy can cause seizures, which can be disruptive to daily life and may require medication or other interventions.

Sleep disorders are also more common in individuals with ASD, and females with ASD are more likely to have sleep disorders compared to males with ASD. Sleep disorders can include difficulty falling asleep, staying asleep, or waking up too early. Sleep disorders can significantly impact daytime functioning, including mood, behavior, and cognitive performance.

Allergies are another co-occurring medical condition that can impact the health of individuals with ASD. Females with ASD are more likely to have allergies compared to males with ASD. Allergies can cause a range of symptoms, including sneezing, runny nose, itchy eyes, and skin rashes.

It is important for healthcare providers to understand the healthcare and medical needs of females with ASD in order to provide appropriate care. This can be challenging, as individuals with ASD may have difficulty communicating their symptoms or may experience sensory processing difficulties in medical settings. However, there are several strategies that can help healthcare providers meet the needs of females with ASD.

One important strategy is to provide a supportive and sensory-friendly environment in medical settings. This can include reducing sensory stimuli, such as bright lights or loud noises, providing comfortable seating, and using calming techniques, such as deep breathing or visualization. Healthcare providers can also use visual supports, such as pictures or diagrams, to help individuals with ASD understand medical procedures and communicate their needs.

Another important strategy is to involve the family or caregivers in the healthcare process. Family members or caregivers can provide important information about the individual's medical history, symptoms, and treatment needs. They can also provide support and comfort during medical procedures and appointments.

It is also important to individualize healthcare plans to meet the specific needs of each individual with ASD. This may involve incorporating sensory strategies, such as providing a weighted blanket or using aromatherapy, into medical procedures. It may also involve working with a multidisciplinary team of healthcare providers, including occupational therapists, speech therapists, and nutritionists, to address co-occurring medical conditions and support overall health and wellness.

Finally, it is important to prioritize healthcare access and affordability for individuals with ASD. This can be challenging, as individuals with ASD may have difficulty accessing healthcare services or may face discrimination in healthcare settings. Healthcare providers and policymakers can work together to address these challenges by promoting healthcare equity and increasing awareness of the healthcare needs of individuals with ASD.

Importance of Early Intervention

Early intervention is key to addressing the healthcare needs of females with ASD. Early diagnosis and intervention can help individuals with ASD access the appropriate medical care and support they need to thrive. It can also prevent the onset or worsening of co-occurring medical conditions and improve overall quality of life.

Early intervention can involve a range of medical and therapeutic interventions, including medication, behavioral therapies, and speech and occupational therapies. It is important to individualize early intervention plans to meet the specific needs of each individual with ASD and to involve the family or caregivers in the intervention process.

Importance of Comprehensive Care

Comprehensive care is essential to meeting the healthcare needs of females with ASD. This involves addressing not only the medical needs of individuals with ASD but also their social, emotional, and developmental needs. Comprehensive care can involve a range of interventions, including mental health services, social skills training, and education and vocational support.

Mental health services are an important component of comprehensive care for females with ASD, as they can help address co-occurring mental health conditions, such as anxiety and depression. Social skills training can help individuals with ASD develop the skills they need to navigate social interactions and build relationships. Education and vocational support can help individuals with ASD access the education and training they need to succeed in school and the workforce.

Chapter 15: Diet and Nutrition

Diet and nutrition are essential components of overall health and well-being, and individuals with autism are no exception. In recent years, there has been growing recognition of the importance of addressing diet and nutrition in the management of autism symptoms. This chapter will provide an overview of the role of diet and nutrition in autism, common nutritional deficiencies in individuals with autism, and strategies for promoting a healthy diet.

The Role of Diet and Nutrition in Autism

The link between diet and autism has been a topic of much debate and research. While there is no consensus on the role of diet in causing or treating autism, there is growing evidence that diet and nutrition can play a significant role in the management of autism symptoms.

One theory is that certain foods or nutrients may exacerbate or contribute to autism symptoms in some individuals. For example, some studies have suggested that gluten and casein, two proteins commonly found in wheat and dairy products, may contribute to gastrointestinal issues and behavioral problems in some individuals with autism.

On the other hand, there is also evidence that a healthy diet and proper nutrition can improve overall health and well-being in individuals with autism. For example, research has shown that some children with autism have nutritional deficiencies in key vitamins and minerals, such as vitamin D, calcium, and magnesium, which can impact their physical and mental health.

Common Nutritional Deficiencies in Individuals with Autism

There are several reasons why individuals with autism may be at higher risk for nutritional deficiencies. For example, some individuals with autism have sensory sensitivities or aversions to certain foods, which can limit their dietary choices. Additionally, some individuals with autism may have gastrointestinal issues, such as irritable bowel syndrome or celiac disease, which can impact nutrient absorption.

One common nutritional deficiency in individuals with autism is vitamin D. Vitamin D is important for bone health, immune function, and overall health and well-being. Research has shown that many individuals with autism have low levels of vitamin D, which can contribute to a range of health issues.

Another common nutritional deficiency in individuals with autism is omega-3 fatty acids. Omega-3 fatty acids are essential for brain health and cognitive function, and research has shown that many children with autism have low levels of these important nutrients. Some studies have suggested that supplementing with omega-3 fatty acids may improve cognitive function and behavior in children with autism.

Strategies for Promoting a Healthy Diet

There are several strategies that can be used to promote a healthy diet and proper nutrition in individuals with autism. These strategies include:

1. Nutritional Counseling: Working with a registered dietitian or nutritionist who specializes in autism can be helpful in developing an individualized nutrition plan for individuals with autism. A nutritionist can help identify nutrient deficiencies and develop strategies for improving nutrient intake.

2. Food Sensory Integration Therapy: Some individuals with autism have sensory sensitivities that make it difficult for them to tolerate certain foods. Food sensory integration therapy is a technique that can be used to help individuals with autism become more comfortable with a wider range of foods.

3. Elimination Diets: Elimination diets involve removing certain foods or food groups from an individual's diet to see if symptoms improve. This can be helpful in identifying food sensitivities or intolerances that may be exacerbating autism symptoms.

4. Supplementing with Vitamins and Minerals: In some cases, supplementing with vitamins and minerals may be necessary to address nutrient deficiencies in individuals with autism. However, it is important to work with a healthcare provider or nutritionist to ensure that supplements are used safely and effectively.

5. Encouraging a Balanced Diet: Encouraging a balanced diet that includes a variety of nutrient-dense foods is important for promoting overall health and well-being in individuals with autism. This can include a variety of fruits, vegetables, lean proteins.

6. Providing Texture and Sensory Variety: Texture and sensory preferences can be a significant challenge for individuals with autism. Providing a variety of textures and sensory experiences can help individuals with autism become more comfortable with different foods and develop a more balanced and varied diet.

7. Encouraging Family Meals: Family meals can be an important opportunity to model healthy eating behaviors and promote positive social interaction. Encouraging family meals can also help ensure that individuals with autism have access to a wide range of healthy foods.

8. Addressing Gastrointestinal Issues: Addressing gastrointestinal issues, such as constipation or diarrhea, can be an important component of promoting a healthy diet in individuals with autism. Working with a healthcare provider or nutritionist to identify and address gastrointestinal issues can help improve nutrient absorption and overall health.

It is important to note that every individual with autism is unique, and there is no one-size-fits-all approach to diet and nutrition. It is important to work with a healthcare provider or nutritionist to develop an individualized plan that takes into account an individual's specific needs and preferences.

Chapter 16: Medications and Treatments for Autism in Females

Autism is a complex neurodevelopmental disorder that affects individuals differently. There is no known cure for autism, but there are various medications and treatments that can help manage the symptoms associated with the condition. In this chapter, we will discuss the different medications and treatments available for females with autism, including their efficacy, risks, and benefits.

Medications for Autism in Females

There are currently no medications specifically designed to treat autism. However, there are certain medications that can be used to manage the symptoms associated with the condition. The most commonly prescribed medications for females with autism are:

Antidepressants: Antidepressants are commonly used to treat depression, anxiety, and other mood disorders that often co-occur with autism. These medications work by regulating neurotransmitters in the brain that affect mood and emotions. Selective serotonin reuptake inhibitors (SSRIs) are the most commonly prescribed antidepressants for females with autism. Studies have shown that SSRIs can help reduce repetitive behaviors, social withdrawal, and anxiety in individuals with autism.

Antipsychotics: Antipsychotics are typically used to treat psychotic disorders such as schizophrenia and bipolar disorder. However, they can also be used to treat irritability, aggression, and other behavioral problems associated with autism. Atypical antipsychotics, such as risperidone and aripiprazole, are the most commonly prescribed antipsychotics for individuals with autism. While these medications have been shown to be effective in reducing symptoms of aggression, irritability, and self-injurious behavior in some individuals with autism, they can also cause side effects such as weight gain, drowsiness, and movement disorders.

Stimulants: Stimulants, such as methylphenidate and amphetamines, are commonly used to treat attention deficit hyperactivity disorder (ADHD) in individuals with autism. These medications work by increasing the levels of dopamine and norepinephrine in the brain, which can improve attention, concentration, and hyperactivity. However, stimulants can also cause side effects such as insomnia, loss of appetite, and irritability.

Mood stabilizers: Mood stabilizers, such as lithium and valproate, are typically used to treat bipolar disorder. However, they can also be used to treat mood swings, aggression, and impulsivity in individuals with autism. While mood stabilizers have been shown to be effective in reducing symptoms of mood instability and aggression in some individuals with autism, they can also cause side effects such as tremors, weight gain, and kidney problems.

It is important to note that while medications can be helpful in managing symptoms of autism in some individuals, they are not a cure for the condition. Medications should always be prescribed and monitored by a qualified healthcare professional, as they can have serious side effects and interactions with other medications.

Treatments for Autism in Females

There are also various treatments available for females with autism that can help improve their quality of life and reduce the severity of their symptoms. The most common treatments for autism include:

Behavioral therapy: Behavioral therapy is a type of therapy that focuses on modifying behavior by reinforcing positive behaviors and reducing negative behaviors. Behavioral therapy is often used to teach individuals with autism social skills, communication, and daily living skills. This therapy can be provided in a group or individual setting and is typically delivered by a trained therapist.

Speech and language therapy: Speech and language therapy is a type of therapy that focuses on improving communication skills in individuals with autism. This therapy can be provided in a group or individual setting and is typically delivered by a licensed speech therapist. Speech and language therapy can help individuals with autism improve their language skills, articulation, and social communication.

Occupational therapy: Occupational therapy is a type of therapy that focuses on helping individuals with autism develop skills that will allow them to participate in daily activities, such as self-care and leisure activities. Occupational therapy can also help individuals with autism develop sensory integration skills, which can help them better understand and manage sensory information.

Sensory integration therapy: Sensory integration therapy is a type of therapy that focuses on helping individuals with autism better understand and manage sensory information. This therapy can involve activities such as brushing the skin, wearing weighted vests, and swinging on a swing. Sensory integration therapy can help individuals with autism better manage sensory information and reduce sensory overload.

Applied Behavior Analysis (ABA) Therapy: ABA therapy is a type of therapy that focuses on improving behaviors and social skills in individuals with autism through positive reinforcement. ABA therapy is typically delivered by a trained therapist in a one-on-one setting and can be effective in improving social skills, communication, and daily living skills.

Dietary interventions: Some individuals with autism may benefit from dietary interventions, such as a gluten-free or casein-free diet. While there is limited scientific evidence to support the effectiveness of dietary interventions for autism, some individuals with autism have reported improvements in symptoms such as gastrointestinal problems, hyperactivity, and irritability after implementing these diets.

It is important to note that there is no one-size-fits-all treatment for autism, and what works for one individual may not work for another. Treatment plans for autism should be individualized and tailored to the specific needs and strengths of the individual.

<u>**Chapter 17: Autism and Pregnancy**</u>

Pregnancy and childbirth can be a time of joy, excitement, and stress for many women, but for those with autism, it can present additional challenges. Autism is a developmental disorder that affects social interaction, communication, and behavior. Although autism is typically diagnosed in childhood, many individuals may not receive a diagnosis until later in life. This means that some women with autism may not be aware of their condition before becoming pregnant.

Challenges Faced by Females with Autism During Pregnancy and Childbirth

There are several challenges that women with autism may face during pregnancy and childbirth. These challenges can include difficulties with communication, sensory sensitivities, and social interactions.

One of the most significant challenges that women with autism may face is communicating with healthcare providers. Many women with autism struggle with verbal communication and may have difficulty expressing their needs and concerns to healthcare providers. This can lead to misunderstandings and a lack of appropriate care.

Sensory sensitivities can also present challenges during pregnancy and childbirth. Many women with autism have heightened sensitivity to sensory stimuli such as light, noise, and touch. This can make the hospital environment overwhelming and uncomfortable.

Social interactions can also be challenging for women with autism during pregnancy and childbirth. They may struggle to navigate social interactions with healthcare providers and family members, and may not feel comfortable with physical touch or displays of affection.

Prenatal Care and Support

Prenatal care is essential for the health and well-being of both mother and baby. However, for women with autism, accessing appropriate prenatal care can be challenging. Healthcare providers may not have experience working with individuals with autism, and may not be aware of their unique needs.

To address this issue, it is important to provide education and training for healthcare providers on how to work effectively with individuals with autism. This can include training on effective communication strategies, sensory sensitivities, and social interactions.

In addition to providing appropriate medical care, women with autism may also require additional support during pregnancy. This can include support from family members or friends, or from support groups for individuals with autism. It is important to recognize that women with autism may require additional emotional and social support during pregnancy and childbirth.

Childbirth and Postpartum Care

Childbirth can be a stressful and overwhelming experience for anyone, but for women with autism, it can be particularly challenging. Women with autism may struggle with the physical and emotional demands of childbirth, and may experience sensory overload in the hospital environment.

It is important for healthcare providers to be aware of these challenges and to provide appropriate support during childbirth. This can include creating a calm and quiet environment, minimizing sensory stimuli, and providing clear and concise communication.

Postpartum care is also essential for the health and well-being of both mother and baby. Women with autism may require additional support during the postpartum period, including support with breastfeeding and bonding with their baby. It is important for healthcare providers to be aware of these needs and to provide appropriate support.

Parenting a Child with Autism

For women with autism who have children, parenting can present additional challenges. Autism is a genetic disorder, which means that there is a higher likelihood that a child of a parent with autism will also have the disorder. This can present unique challenges in parenting, including difficulties with communication and social interactions.

It is important for parents with autism to receive appropriate support and resources to help them navigate the challenges of parenting a child with autism. This can include support groups, educational resources, and access to therapy and other services.

<u>**Chapter 18: Legal and Ethical Considerations**</u>

Individuals with autism face a range of legal and ethical considerations that can impact their ability to access education, employment, and other opportunities. These considerations are particularly relevant for females with autism, who face unique challenges and barriers in these areas. In this chapter, we will explore some of the legal and ethical considerations related to autism in females, and the importance of advocacy and awareness in addressing these issues.

Discrimination in Employment and Education

One of the most significant legal and ethical considerations facing individuals with autism is discrimination in employment and education. Females with autism are often overlooked for opportunities or face barriers to accessing them due to discriminatory practices. This can include everything from hiring managers who are hesitant to hire someone with autism to teachers who do not provide appropriate accommodations in the classroom.

Discrimination can occur at any stage of the employment or education process, from recruitment to performance evaluations. In some cases, individuals with autism may face discrimination based on assumptions about their abilities or limitations, without consideration of their skills, qualifications, or potential. This can lead to missed opportunities for growth and development, as well as a lack of support for individuals with autism to achieve their goals and pursue their passions.

Legal Protections and Accommodations

Fortunately, there are legal protections and accommodations in place to help address discrimination against individuals with autism. In the UK, the Equality Act 2010 provides protections against discrimination on the basis of disability, including autism. This means that employers and educators are required to make reasonable adjustments to ensure that individuals with autism can access the same opportunities as their neurotypical peers. Reasonable adjustments might include things like providing extra time on exams, offering support in the workplace, or providing assistive technology to help with communication or sensory needs.

Additionally, there are various organisations and advocacy groups that can offer support and resources for individuals with autism and their families. The National Autistic Society, for example, offers guidance on topics like employment, education, and housing, as well as advice and support for individuals with autism and their families.

Legal protections and accommodations can be powerful tools for addressing discrimination against individuals with autism, but they are not always enough on their own. In many cases, advocacy and awareness are also critical components of promoting inclusion and supporting individuals with autism.

Importance of Advocacy and Awareness

Advocacy and awareness are important for a range of reasons. Firstly, they can help to combat stigma and discrimination against individuals with autism. By raising awareness about the unique challenges and strengths of individuals with autism, we can help to break down barriers and promote inclusion.

Advocacy can also help to ensure that individuals with autism have access to the resources and support they need to thrive. This might include things like educational or vocational support, mental health services, or access to therapies and interventions that can help to improve quality of life.

Another important aspect of advocacy and awareness is the need for ongoing research and development in the field of autism. While we have made significant progress in recent years, there is still much to learn about autism and its impact on individuals, particularly females. Ongoing research can help to identify new treatments and interventions, as well as shed light on the unique challenges and strengths of individuals with autism.

Promising New Therapies and Interventions

There are a range of promising new therapies and interventions being developed for individuals with autism. These include things like behavioural interventions, medication, and assistive technology. For example, virtual reality therapy is a relatively new approach that uses technology to simulate real-world scenarios in a controlled environment, allowing individuals with autism to practice social skills and other behaviours in a safe and supportive setting.

Other therapies focus on addressing specific symptoms or challenges associated with autism, such as sensory processing difficulties. Sensory integration therapy, for example, aims to help individuals with autism to better process and integrate sensory information, leading to improved communication, behaviour, and emotional regulation.

Future Directions

Looking to the future, there is much work to be done to improve the lives of individuals with autism, particularly females. We need continued advocacy and awareness, as well as ongoing research and development in the field of autism. This will require collaboration between researchers, healthcare providers, policymakers, and advocacy groups, as well as individuals with autism and their families.

One promising area of research is the development of new diagnostic tools and methods that can help to identify autism in females more accurately. This may include changes to diagnostic criteria or the development of new assessment tools that are specifically tailored to the unique challenges and strengths of females with autism.

Another important area of research is the need for more personalised and individualised interventions for individuals with autism. This might involve tailoring therapies and supports to the specific needs and strengths of each individual, as well as considering the unique social and cultural contexts in which they live.

Chapter 19: Research and Future Directions

Over the past few decades, there has been a growing awareness of the unique challenges faced by females with autism. However, research into autism has historically focused on males, leading to a lack of understanding of the experiences and needs of females with autism. In recent years, there has been a push for more research into autism in females, and promising new findings have emerged.

Current Research on Autism in Females

One area of research that has received significant attention in recent years is the gender differences in autism symptom presentation. Studies have found that females with autism may exhibit different patterns of behavior than males with autism, which may contribute to their underdiagnosis or misdiagnosis. For example, females with autism may have better social communication skills, but struggle with social interaction and understanding social cues. They may also have more restricted interests and repetitive behaviors than males with autism. This highlights the importance of considering gender differences when assessing and diagnosing autism in females.

Another area of research that has gained attention is the co-occurring conditions in females with autism. Research has found that females with autism are more likely to have comorbid conditions such as anxiety, depression, and eating disorders than males with autism. This suggests that addressing co-occurring conditions is a crucial component of treatment for females with autism.

Furthermore, studies have found that females with autism may experience more emotional and psychological challenges than males with autism. For example, females with autism may be at a higher risk of developing anxiety, depression, and suicidal ideation. They may also experience social isolation and difficulties forming meaningful relationships. Addressing these challenges is critical to improving the quality of life for females with autism.

The Importance of Including Females in Autism Research

The underrepresentation of females in autism research has been a longstanding issue, but it is now being addressed. As more studies are conducted on autism in females, researchers are discovering new insights into the unique experiences and needs of females with autism. For example, research has found that females with autism may have a higher risk of developing self-injurious behaviors, which can have significant implications for treatment and support.

Including females in autism research is also essential for developing more effective treatments and interventions. Historically, treatments for autism have been developed based on studies conducted predominantly on males with autism. However, research has found that females with autism may respond differently to treatments than males with autism. For example, studies have found that females with autism may have a higher response to behavioral and educational interventions than medication-based treatments.

Promising New Therapies and Interventions

As more research is conducted on autism in females, promising new therapies and interventions are being developed. For example, studies have found that cognitive-behavioral therapy (CBT) can be an effective treatment for anxiety in females with autism. CBT is a type of therapy that focuses on changing negative thoughts and behaviors and replacing them with positive ones.

Another promising intervention for females with autism is social skills training. Studies have found that social skills training can be effective in improving social interaction and communication in females with autism. Social skills training involves teaching individuals with autism specific social skills, such as initiating and maintaining conversations, reading nonverbal cues, and making eye contact.

Furthermore, research has also shown that early intervention is crucial for improving outcomes for individuals with autism. Early diagnosis and intervention can help address challenges and support the development of important skills such as social communication, behavior management, and self-regulation.

In addition to traditional therapies and interventions, technology-based interventions are also being developed to support individuals with autism. For example, wearable devices and smartphone apps can be used to support social interaction and communication, and virtual reality technology can be used to provide a safe and controlled environment for social skills training.

Areas for Future Research and Development

While progress has been made in research into autism in females, there is still much to be learned. One area for future research is the development of more accurate and reliable diagnostic tools for females with autism. Current diagnostic criteria for autism were developed based on studies conducted predominantly on males, and may not fully capture the unique symptom presentation of females with autism. Developing more sensitive and accurate diagnostic tools can help ensure that females with autism are diagnosed and receive appropriate support and interventions.

Another area for future research is the exploration of the biological and genetic factors that contribute to autism in females. While there is evidence that genetics play a role in the development of autism, the specific genetic and biological mechanisms are not fully understood. Understanding the biological and genetic underpinnings of autism in females can help inform the development of more effective treatments and interventions.

Finally, there is a need for research into the long-term outcomes of females with autism. While early intervention can improve outcomes, little is known about the long-term outcomes for females with autism. Studying the long-term outcomes of females with autism can help inform the development of support and services that meet the needs of individuals with autism across the lifespan.

<u>**Chapter 20: Conclusion and Call to Action**</u>

The previous chapters have highlighted the unique challenges faced by females with autism and the importance of understanding and addressing these challenges from a UK medical viewpoint. It is clear that autism affects females differently than males, and it is crucial that we recognize and respond to these differences in our approach to diagnosis, treatment, and support.

Despite the growing awareness of autism in recent years, there is still much work to be done in improving the lives of individuals with autism, especially females. While early diagnosis and intervention can greatly improve outcomes for individuals with autism, there are still many barriers that prevent females from accessing timely and appropriate care.

One of the biggest challenges is the lack of recognition and understanding of autism in females, both among healthcare professionals and the general public. Many females with autism are misdiagnosed or undiagnosed altogether, and they may face discrimination or lack of support in educational or employment settings.

Additionally, the co-occurring conditions that are common in individuals with autism, such as anxiety and depression, can further complicate the picture for females. They may struggle with emotional regulation and social interactions, leading to social isolation and other negative outcomes.

To address these challenges and improve the lives of females with autism, we need a multi-faceted approach that includes education, advocacy, and research. We need to increase awareness and understanding of autism in females, both among healthcare professionals and the general public. This can include targeted campaigns and educational programs that highlight the unique challenges faced by females with autism and the importance of early identification and intervention.

We also need to advocate for policy changes and legal protections that support individuals with autism, including females. This can include anti-discrimination legislation and policies that require schools and employers to provide reasonable accommodations for individuals with autism.

Finally, we need to prioritize research into autism in females, both to better understand the condition and to develop more effective treatments and interventions. This can include studies that explore the unique neurodevelopmental differences in females with autism, as well as clinical trials of new therapies and medications.

Despite the challenges that individuals with autism, especially females, face, there is reason for hope. Many individuals with autism go on to lead happy and fulfilling lives, and with the right support and interventions, individuals with autism can achieve their full potential.

It is important to remember that each individual with autism is unique, and that treatment and support must be individualized to meet their specific needs. Some individuals may benefit from medication, while others may benefit from behavioral therapy or other interventions. The key is to provide comprehensive, individualized care that addresses the full range of challenges faced by individuals with autism.

END

Thank you for taking the time to read this Introduction to a Neurodiverse World book.
We have a range of books within this series that are steadily being released.
Topics Cover

- Autism
- ADHD
- Sensory Processing Disorder (SPD)
- Pathological Demand Avoidance (PDA)
- Avoidant Restrictive Food Intake Disorder (ARFID)
- PICA

We also post weekly Articles on our website and our social media sites (links Below)

Divergent Consultants Ltd are accredited Counsellors and Psychotherapists who specialise in Spectrum Disorders.

Started by Gareth Croot when his 3-year-old Non-Verbal son was diagnosed with Autism Spectrum Disorder, Global Development Delay and Hypermobility.
This lead his family on a journey resulting in his 12 year old daughter starting the ASD diagnostic pathway and Gareth also being diagnosed with Autism, PDA, Hypermobility and currently awaiting ADHD assessment.
Divergent Consultants offer introduction to Autism Courses, Sleep Therapy Courses, Pre and Post diagnosis counselling for parents and newly diagnosed adults aswell as general support functions
you can visit us at www.divergentconsultants.co.uk
Facebook https://www.facebook.com/people/Divergent-Consultants/100088643106730/
TikTok https://www.tiktok.com/divergentconsultants
Instagram
https://www.instagram.com/divergent_consultants/